12 HOMESCHOOL MYTHS
DEBUNKED

12 HOMESCHOOL MYTHS DEBUNKED

The Book for Skeptical Dads

KENT LARSON

ROGUE SCHOOL PRESS

12 Homeschool Myths Debunked
Copyright © 2018 by Kent Larson

ISBN: 978-0-9983856-4-8 (softcover)
ISBN: 978-0-9983856-5-5 (ebook)

Large scale education was not developed to motivate kids or to create scholars. It was invented to churn out adults who worked well within the system.

Seth Godin

Contents

Foreword

Finally, a book about homeschooling written for dads! In particular, this book is written for dads who may be skeptical about homeschooling. Perhaps your wife has suggested it, and you have questions and concerns. Maybe you are not satisfied with the education your child is receiving in a public or private school and would like to learn about other options. Perhaps you are disquieted about the social interaction, bullying or values at your child's school. There are many reasons families investigate homeschooling. This book will help you to make a more informed decision.

Kent Larson does a superb job taking a look at 12 of the most prevalent myths about homeschooling and assessing if there is validity to them. In a friendly and conversational manner, he logically breaks them down casting upon research and his own personal experiences to enlighten the reader about this rapidly growing form of education.

While Kent wrote this book for dads, it is also an excellent read for anyone considering homeschooling or for someone in a homeschooling family's life who is skeptical about their decision. With loads of curriculum options as well as so many opportunities for kids to engage in their communities and explore their passions, contemporary homeschooling is the ultimate choice in providing your child a customized education.

I am also honored to call Kent a good friend. Both our families love homeschooling and are grateful that we took the gamble to see if it was a good fit for us. It turned out to be, and we enjoy watching our kids thrive intellectually, emotionally and socially. Kent is a very engaged dad. The love, time and effort he puts into his kids is evidenced in his kids themselves. His son is in 7th grade and daughter in 4th grade. Talented, mature, intelligent, articulate and respectful, Kent's children are wonderful examples of homeschool kids with purposeful and engaged parents.

Lastly, I ask many parents considering homeschooling what do they have to lose by giving it a shot. If it doesn't work out, you can always go back. However, you may be missing out on one of the most important choices for your family if you never try. So many parents I have talked to told me they wish they would have started sooner.

The Contemporary Homeschooler (.com)

Start Here

This is a book for dads.

In particular, it's a book for dads who are skeptical about homeschooling. I know something about this topic because I too was a skeptical dad.

For me, homeschooling was out of the question — not even worthy of investigation. I could quickly recite a laundry list of "reasons" why homeschooling was a stupid idea, and I genuinely believed every one of them. The education of my kids was serious business, best left to professionals. Homeschool, really?! I wasn't about to let my family become lab rats in some fringe social experiment!

I reacted this way because I genuinely believed many of the prevalent myths surrounding homeschooling — many of which you probably believe too. In hindsight, I realize that I believed them primarily for two reasons: first, they were often repeated and considered "common wisdom," and secondly, they fit my bias. What bias? That the process of education was best left to the professionals. My natural conclusion was to categorically dismiss the idea of homeschooling because it was not worthy of consideration.

Then something changed. I discovered that some of the myths I'd believed were false. I assured myself, however, the "other reasons" were still sufficient to justify dismissing the topic. But then I began discovering many of these were not true either. At some point in my journey, I realized that I needed to thoughtfully examine each of my "reasons" to be sure they were at least partly based on fact. I ultimately concluded most were merely myths that, with a bit of investigation, were quickly debunked.

I wish there had been a single, bottom-line resource to turn to at the start of my journey. It would have saved me a ton of time and anxiety. That's why I wrote this book. I've designed it to be a quick read that cuts to the chase and candidly addresses the fears surrounding homeschooling. Eliminating false beliefs is the first step to understanding the topic and is the sole focus of this book.

I'm not going to try to convince you that homeschooling is the best thing for your family. That's a decision only you can make. This book will merely remove the obstacles to making an *informed decision* regarding the many education options available to your family.

This book will NOT

- Try to sell you on homeschooling
- Provide how-to information
- Bore you with tons of details

This book will

- Candidly and honestly address each myth
- Be a quick read
- Maintain a big-picture focus

I encourage you to read the Introduction, to see where I'm coming from and how my perspective changed. Then feel free to jump directly to the myths that concern you most. I do encourage you to read them all at some point because many of the myths are related and derive from similar underlying fears or misunderstandings. But you're in the driver's seat — with this book as you are for your kids' education.

Introduction

There was just no way I would ever allow my kids to be homeschooled. Not a possibility! There was too much at stake, and I wanted the absolute best for them. The best opportunities, training, experiences, and friends. After all, I had been entrusted with the lives of two incredibly smart, creative, talented kids who could accomplish anything, and it was my job as their dad to make sure I didn't screw them up!

If you're a skeptical dad with genuine concerns about the validity and effectiveness of homeschooling, then you're in the right place. I wrote this book for you because I shared those same concerns. My skepticism and fears resulted from a collection of commonly held myths and fallacies surrounding this topic. I'll explain as we proceed just how these myths began to fall, one after the other, and why I subsequently pivoted from skeptical dad to home-schooling advocate.

I had heard about homeschooling but didn't give it much thought since it conjured up images of odd, isolated kids with hillbilly parents. I wanted no part of that! I dismissed the notion and didn't perform any type of due diligence to understand what homeschooling *really was,* and what it *could be.* It was easier and more comfortable for me to just believe the many myths and stereotypes than to actually find out the truth. So, for a time, I continued to do what everyone else was doing.

Besides, we were already quite invested in our kids' education well before they were even born. My wife and I had kids later in life and had already been paying into the US and California education systems via taxation for two decades. Upon having kids, we moved to a great kid-oriented community that had excellent public schools. We paid a lot to live there, but it was worth it since we were close to a good school. Communities with good, safe schools are more expensive. So, before our kids ever attended kindergarten, their "free" public school education had already cost us quite a bit!

You're probably thinking that at some point early on in our kids' education things must have taken a turn for the worse, driving us to homeschool out of desperation. But that wasn't the case for us. In fact, our son had a good experience in our local public school system. He had competent, caring teachers and a good group of friends.

Our son was learning, and in many ways, thriving. So why in the world would we pull him out and start homeschooling? It's a fair question.

The homeschooling option sounds absurd, especially to dads. This is based primarily on the fear that it might harm our kids. But if we're honest, the fear of what others will think also plays a part. I get it! I didn't want to look like a kook either, particularly to friends and family. If the myths were true, then anyone who homeschooled their kids must be a kook! But the truth changes everything. The real kooks are the ones who aren't willing to look and listen to anything new or different, embracing only the comfortable and familiar instead of the truth. That's a bold statement, but one that I bet most guys would agree with. I will be brutally honest throughout this book, and I won't pull punches. You can rest assured, *I'm not trying to sell you on homeschooling.* I also don't believe that dads who choose the traditional route love their kids any less!

As mentioned, I have the same concerns and fears as anyone else. I desperately want the best for my kids, and I certainly don't want them to be weird! Much like you, I desire to raise well-rounded, competent, cool, creative, and athletic kids who will have a rich childhood and teen years, develop great friendships, and have life-enriching experiences. It's always been important to me that they get into a good college, achieve career success, and have an overall great life. The question is: which education path provides the best odds of achieving these goals?

I knew first-hand how the "traditional education" model worked. I was a product of it. It's very predictable, and thus appealing to most people. It gives us some control over the outcome (or at least the illusion of control). Our children enter via kindergarten and exit the other end as high school graduates. They walk away with a diploma certifying that their education has included basic academic knowledge in standard subjects and their proficiency in these subjects has been vetted by an independent third party. This is a system designed to consistently produce specific results (which it mostly does). So why upset the applecart? Heck, I'm a product of the traditional, group-school model and still turned out okay. But did I turn out okay *because* of the traditional school model, or *despite* it? Just because we survived, perhaps even thrived, doesn't mean our experience was optimal.

Like life itself, my education was a collection of both positive and negative experiences, influences, ideas, and relationships. This reality led me to conclude that there is no *perfect* way to do education. The traditional model is society's best attempt at providing education services to a large and disparate population of kids. It's a noble effort to be sure but not perfect. In my mind, however, I treated it as though it was the only viable option. It was only later that I started to ask more questions.

As I began to investigate homeschooling, in earnest, I found an overwhelming number of books, websites, and resources available (some quite good, some not), but there was nothing that directly addressed my concerns *as a dad.* I hope this book will. I want to provide straight, honest answers to the questions and concerns of men. While we may share many of the same concerns as our wives, chances are we weigh them differently.

Most of my worries were eventually addressed by talking with homeschool families, fellow dads in particular. After much research, lengthy discussions, and a fair amount of anxiety, my wife and I chose the homeschool option.

I admit that *I didn't want* to arrive at this conclusion! Frankly, I didn't want the responsibility. *I didn't want* homeschooling to be a viable option for my family, but it became increasingly difficult to deny it was. Realizing this took time. Like I mentioned, most of the myths I had believed were debunked through conversations with homeschool families — mainly other men. The fact that these homeschool dads were onboard with this "lunacy" got my attention. These dads weren't a bunch of wimps whose wives badgered them into some type of emasculated acquiescence! No, these were smart, accomplished, real men who had embraced homeschooling wholeheartedly and had become advocates.

I'm not in a position to say whether the homeschooling option is best for your family. I'll state confidently, however, that you *must make an informed decision about your kids' education* — one based on reality, not fables.

Before we launch into the 12 myths, I want to mention

a real pet peeve of mine – the word "homeschool." I hate this word! It doesn't describe anything I want for my kids. First, the words "home" and "school" do not belong together. Home should be a sanctuary – not a school. It's already bad enough that we have "home-work" but an entire day of school at home sounds like hell to me. Second, there's an implied antisocial aspect to the term that conjures images of isolated kooks in a backwoods cabin who have completely withdrawn from society. I suspect you've likely envisioned something similar. The name itself gives rise to all sorts of misconceptions and stereotypes – or at the very least fans the flames. By the end of this book, I hope you'll agree that the name does not describe the experience!

Let's jump right in. Grab a beer and a comfortable chair and let's debunk the myths about homeschooling!

Myths About Harm to Kids

ONE

What About Socialization?

LET'S START with the mother of all fears about home-schooling: *socialization*. In fact, whenever the word "home-school" is uttered, the knee-jerk reaction of everyone within earshot is to express concern about "socialization" – whatever that means. I find it comical that the topic of homeschooling causes people to start speaking as if they've earned a Ph.D. in Child Psychology! It turns out that the feared lack of "socialization" means different things to different people. For skeptical dads, it generally means the following:

- Kids will become isolated, inside at home all day
- Kids won't develop interpersonal skills or friendships

- Kids will turn out to be socially inept, goofy, awkward, and nerdy

I fully acknowledge that socialization is an essential factor in our kids' development. As dads, we want our kids to be well-adjusted, well-equipped, cool even, and properly socialized! But we skeptical dads are convinced that without the influences of other kids, teachers, and coaches our kids will not be equipped for life in the real world. I understand that fear and felt the same way. Thankfully, homeschooling does *not* lack those crucial ingredients, nor does it result in a lack of socialization. At least, it need not — more on that shortly.

My eyes were opened to the fallacy of the "socialization argument" early in my homeschooling investigation when I was speaking to a good friend of mine, himself a home-school dad. I dropped this "mother of all anti-homeschool bombshells," then self-righteously sat back to see how my friend would respond. Confidently I asked, "well, what about socialization?" I hoped to watch him squirm in his seat, naively assuming he wouldn't have thought about this objection before. To my surprise, and without missing a beat, he responded with a question of his own (one that I now pose to you): "Do you really want your kid socialized by a mob of unruly 3rd graders?" Now, depending on which grades your kids are in currently, you can substitute that in the above question. I suspect that if your kids are in junior high or even high school, you may answer even more emphatically in the negative than I did! I was the one who ultimately squirmed in my seat replying, "well, of course not."

Of course, skeptical dads are not merely suggesting that dumping kids into a 3rd grade classroom will lead to socialization. They aren't proposing a *Lord of the Flies* scenario. It's clear the socialization process means something specific. But what exactly?

In the traditional education model, teachers certainly play a crucial role. After all, our kids spend the bulk of their waking hours each school day with their teachers and fellow-students. Remaining time at home is increasingly spent heads-down on homework. As our kids get older and progress through the school system, our day-to-day influence (at least in the socialization of our kids) will decrease. Sure, teachers, coaches, church youth leaders, and other parents can all have a significant positive impact on our kids' development. These can present good and necessary inputs to their socialization – we all agree on this point. But I have found this same type of input, the valuable part of the "socialization process," is very much present in the homeschooling world. I would even say that homeschooling presents opportunities for socialization in significantly *enhanced* ways.

The socialization myth is the strongest of all myths because it's based on several core fears we dads are too quick to embrace. Let's look at some of the underlying assumptions and misconceptions that undergird the social-ization myth.

Isolation

Isolation is the central assumption and fear behind the socialization argument. We assume the homeschooling process would result in our kids (and us as parents to some degree) becoming isolated from the outside world.

Before I knew better, I had assumed some crazy things about homeschooling. In one scenario, I feared that all the people who might positively influence our kids would be banished from their lives, and that we would never leave the house. I envisioned my wife relegated to an unfulfilled life in front of a traditional black slate chalkboard, attempting to teach our bored-to-tears kids. My vision included my wife in a perpetual state of exhaustion, exasperated, hair disheveled, and wearing something from the 1970's TV show *Little House on the Prairie*. Our kids, in my mind at least, had rotted teeth, ill-fitting clothing, and, for some unknown reason, cockney accents! I do admit to having a colorful imagination, but I bet you've pictured something similar regarding homeschooling. Considering the type of oppressive isolation this myth promotes, it's not surprising that many people dismiss the idea outright.

My imagination aside, isolation (and socialization) is a serious concern of all parents. However, the myth that homeschooling results in isolation is not true! *It's almost impossible for kids to emerge from a homeschooled educational experience without proper socialization.* We found that homeschool families have tons of incredible opportunities. So much in fact, that we and others like us are rarely home! We learn alongside other people in our network and are outside of the house most of the time.

Isolation turns out not to be a problem at all. In fact, the more significant concern among homeschool families is how to "balance" all the things we want to do while maintaining a *healthy* amount of margin. We all realize that we can't do everything, but it's hard when there are so many great opportunities. Ultimately, *the single biggest challenge we've faced in homeschooling is to avoid overcommitting!* The truth is there are far more classes, field trips, adventures, and cultural opportunities than any family can possibly do. We want to do them all, *and our kids want to do them too!*

Several times in this book, I will refer to a "co-op" which means a group of families that meet consistently to conduct classes and facilitate educational, creative, and social activities. The classes are typically parent-led although professional teachers are sometimes contracted for specific subjects. Co-ops range from those consisting of just a few families and meeting in homes to those consisting of 100 or more families meeting in commercial facilities. Some of the larger co-ops often resemble traditional schools in many ways, by providing classes in many subjects for kindergarten through high school grades.

Co-ops aren't your only option. Many educational

organizations and vendors cater to homeschoolers by offering classes and workshops. There are field trip groups, music and theater studios, and even club sports organizations that cater to homeschooled students. Most metropolitan areas have a lot of options to choose from. Even in rural communities, active homeschooling groups are common. These various groups can be found quite easily online and in the more active homeschool Facebook groups.

In my experience, joining a co-op is the fastest way to plug into this networked community of fellow homeschoolers. New homeschooling families immediately benefit from the shared experiences of those who are already established. And the kids make friends quickly. My family, for example, is part of a large local co-op, a field trip group, and we also take classes at a local homeschool campus. Our kids are interacting with tons of other kids almost every day of the week. Under these circumstances, isolation and lack of socialization are impossible. Suffice it to say, the myth of isolation is utterly false.

It turns out "community" is one of the most important and valuable aspects of the homeschooling experience. I will have much more to say about this later but know that our kids are outside, experiencing life, learning by doing, gaining life-skills, being challenged and tested, learning to be resourceful, and all the while sharing these experiences and lessons with a large community of equally invested families.

Stifled Relationships and Social Interactions

There is a related myth that homeschoolers won't develop relationships with other kids. This harkens back to the isolation fear we just dispelled, that feeds the fear of limited social interaction and stifled relationships with people outside the family. I suppose there have been some who have used homeschooling of their children as part of a more general withdrawal from society and culture. I have not met these people, ever, in all our years of homeschooling. I'll grant they probably exist somewhere, but that's not the homeschooling world I've encountered. As previously explained, my kids are out in the world with friends almost constantly. Let's explore what this looks like so you can judge for yourself.

When deciding to homeschool, we quickly plugged into a large networked community of homeschool families by joining a local co-op and field trip group. It turned out, much to my surprise, these people were neither unsocialized nor weird. In fact, they really didn't fit *any* of the popular homeschool stereotypes. Strangely, I was almost disappointed! I was so convinced that my assumptions about homeschooling were correct, I was uncomfortable with how wrong I appeared to be.

My kids have tons of friends of all ages. They are experiencing a rich childhood and making deep connections with peers and the families of peers. I, as a parent, get to share in all of this. Most families start homeschooling because they want to give their kids something more – but parents also find community. Don't dismiss the value of this! I know, as guys we're busy and have the weight of the world on our shoulders. I get it that we don't think we need community in the same way as our wives. And I'm embarrassed to admit that while I was glad my wife could plug into a networked community of homeschool parents, I didn't think I needed it. After all, I was busy and not looking for more things to do, or even for people to meet. But as I started to get to know many of the homeschool families, I found that I really liked them, and we had much in common.

Ours is an exciting and diverse group – economically, culturally, ethnically, and professionally. We, as a family, are now quite close with many of the families in our homeschool community and we have a fuller social calendar than ever. I've also become good friends with many of the dads. Shared experiences and values have a way of creating quick bonds. Enough said on this for now.

Social Awkwardness

Now that the isolation and relational fears have been addressed, I think you'll realize there is nothing inherent in homeschooling that hinders experiences or relationships. Our kids are with the other kids in our network multiple days per week. It follows that the homeschooling process doesn't make kids nerdy or socially inept. Are there nerdy homeschool kids? Sure, just like there are nerdy kids in traditional schools. Here's the hard truth: if my kid's a nerd or socially awkward, it's probably because I am. Ouch! Homeschoolers don't have a monopoly on this.

I have noticed more maturity among homeschooling kids – which can sometimes come off as a bit different than other kids their age. But that's not a bad thing. I think this is because homeschooled kids tend to have more interaction with kids of various ages (both older and younger) and more frequent, deeper communication with adults. So, more mature speech patterns can often result. Homeschooled kids also don't typically experience as much negative peer pressure or pressure to conform to cultural trends as their traditionally schooled peers. That's not to say that they are detached or otherwise unaware of trends and culture — just that I've witnessed a more relaxed and accepting attitude among the homeschooled kids overall.

The Empirical Evidence Reaches the Same Conclusion

I understand that some may be skeptical about my experience and observations as perhaps not being representative. Academic studies show self-concept and overall socialization are on average higher for homeschooled kids when measuring homeschooling's effect on socialization. The researchers utilized the respected Piers-Harris Children's Self-Concept Scale (PHSCS) among other tools and concluded:

1. The self-concept of the home-schooling children was significantly higher (p<.001) than that of the conventionally schooled population on the global scale and all six subscales of the PHSCS. On the global scale, half of the home schoolers scored at or above the 91st percentile. This condition may be due to higher achievement and mastery levels, independent study characteristics, or one-on-one tutoring situations in the home-school environment. It could also be due, perhaps, to higher levels of parental interest and communication, peer independence, a sense of responsibility, and lowered anxiety levels.

2. Insofar as self-concept is a reflector of socialization, it would appear that few home-schooling children are socially deprived. Critics of the home school should not urge self-concept and socialization rationales. These factors apparently favor home schoolers over the conventionally schooled population.

Moore Home Schooling : Self-Concept in Home-Schooling Children. Accessed June 27, 2018. http://www.moorefoundation.com/article/49/faqs/self-concept-in-home-schooling-children.

The above conclusions are quite profound. I encourage those who are interested to view the full article since it contains many additional insights.

Bottom Line

In summary, *I was utterly wrong* about homeschooling leading to isolation and stifled peer relationships. The opposite is true! Homeschooling opens the door to a previously unknown world of textured educational and relational opportunities – not just for the kids, but for parents too!

It's also false that homeschooling will cause your kids to become socially awkward. Just like with traditional school, it's on us as dads to help them navigate the social landscape.

How do we ultimately answer the "socialization" question? What is the actual impact of homeschooling on our kids' socialization? Homeschooling, we've found, does not limit socialization at all! Instead, it provides social growth opportunities equal to or greater than any other alternative. Homeschooling, it turns out, *enhances socialization.*

TWO

Can't Play Team Sports

THERE IS a prevalent myth circulating that homeschooled kids miss out on team sports. Skeptical dads often offer up the statement, "But I want my kid to be able to play sports" as a reason not to homeschool. This is a paper tiger. Why? Because organized sports programs have been virtually eliminated at the public elementary and middle school levels. Some private schools still offer programs, but even this is becoming rare. Unless your kids are in high school, why are you worrying about this? If you are thinking about homeschooling your high schoolers, we'll cover some options below.

Many younger kids, homeschoolers included, play in city leagues. More serious players go into club sports. None of this is precluded by homeschooling. In fact, home-schoolers have far more flexibility in their schedules, giving them the ability to devote much more time and energy to their sport. And no more late nights completing hours of homework after practice!

Homeschooling has become a popular option for athletes as well as kids training in the arts. Parents are increasingly choosing to homeschool for the flexibility to devote significant time to training. No longer relegated to just Olympians or child actors, parents are increasingly choosing to homeschool the kids who are showing promise in a variety of areas. This gets around the limitations of traditional school schedules and excessive homework requirements, freeing up the kids to spend time training. While I'm not convinced that this alone is the best reason to homeschool, it does work well for many families. I encourage those who do it for this reason to plug into a local homeschooling community for a richer, more well-rounded experience.

For elementary and middle schoolers, this myth is false.

High School Sports

Many states allow homeschoolers to participate in public high school sports (and be involved in other high school activities too). But not all. As a result, families who home-school at the high school level *don't necessarily* have to give up on the experiences and opportunities that the tradi-tional school system provides — but you'll need to find out how it works from your state athletic association and local school district.

Sadly, this type of equal access does not exist in all states. Using my home state of California as an example, homeschoolers are currently *not allowed* to play high school sports for their local high school. Even charter school students, who are legally considered public school students, are denied access. High school sports in California are governed by the California Interscholastic Federation (CIF) which has stringent and, in this case, discriminatory rules about student eligibility. Even separate homeschool league teams are banned from competing against the public and private high school teams!

If your kid wants to play on their local high school team in a state that doesn't allow it, the only alternative to full-time attendance is to enroll in an independent study program *administered by the same local high school at which the student would play*, if one is available. But then you're not homeschooling, you're just doing all the regular class work at home.

There are some alternatives to the traditional high school sports system, such as separate homeschool leagues and club sports. In California, for example, there is a very active statewide sports organization just for homeschoolers. I'm not suggesting that these options are equivalent to those offered by your states athletic association, which has millions of dollars and decades of tradition behind it. But don't be too quick to dismiss the homeschool leagues as a viable option, I think you'll be surprised by the maturity and breadth of many of these organizations.

In fairness, your kids aren't precluded from playing team sports entirely, as this myth suggests. Instead, they are prevented from playing sports at a public or private high school at which they *are not enrolled*.

Thankfully, some states are more accommodating. At the time of this writing, 22 states in the US allow homeschoolers to play team sports for their local high school and often to participate in additional events and classes too.

Bottom Line

The myth that homeschooling precludes the ability to play team sports is false for elementary and middle school grades because they have the same city league and club opportunities as the traditionally schooled students.

Since homeschooled high school students in some states have the option of playing sports (and other activities) with your local high school, you are free to choose to homeschool if it makes sense for your family without sports being the deciding factor. For these, the myth is false.

But those who live in states that ban homeschoolers from high school sports are forced to make a tough choice. If homeschooling through high school is the best for your kids, then it makes sense to pursue other options for sports, even if they are inferior. For this last group of high schoolers, sadly, the myth is effectively true.

THREE

Academics Will Suffer

ACADEMICS ARE a big concern for everyone who evaluates homeschooling. We are talking about our kids' education, after all. The process that will set them up for success or failure in life. Education is supposed to be the great equalizer. It will make the difference between my kids being able to take care of themselves...and move out of my house...or not. The fear of screwing this up is terrifying. Of course, "education" is much more than just academics, so we need to keep that in perspective. But academics are a part of the overall education process that we dads tend to worry about a lot!

Dads tend to look at the big picture and fear a domino effect of failure. We expect a good K-12 education to enable entry into a good college that then enables obtaining a good job that then enables a good retirement. If we screw up the K-12 part, the dominos fall. Now, it's not really that dire nor are there any guarantees that following the standard model will result in a steady sequence of successes either. Nonetheless, guys tend to think in these terms. Therefore, it makes sense that academic concerns and fears about this cascading effect of failure would present a serious obstacle to doing anything outside of the norm – mainly taking on the personal responsibility for the education of your kids. I get it, and I was very much of the same mindset. In fact, I needed a lot of convincing on this one.

One thing that surprised me when I was first introduced to the homeschooling world was the number of teachers (current and former) who homeschool their own kids. I was shocked. This had to mean they were convinced that better education for their kids could be provided via homeschooling. So that was positive validation, by professional teachers, of homeschooling's potential benefit. But it didn't help *my confidence in doing the same* since I'm not a professional teacher! My initial thought was that they would know how to teach their kids, understand the state requirements, gauge progress, and ensure quality education, but I was certainly in no position to do so. I will cover this topic in more detail in the "I'm Not Equipped to Teach" chapter. For our purposes here, just know I remained doubtful that my wife and I could satisfy the academic needs of our kids. But I was missing a crucial perspective.

You don't need to recreate the classroom! This unique insight empowered us. It sounds simple and obvious, but I had previously thought we would have to recreate the entire school system in our home! We didn't, and neither do you!

Think about why traditional classrooms are organized and operate the way they do. Whether it's a 3rd grade class or a high school class, the classroom is designed to solve a logistics problem. For the sake of argument let's say there are 28 students and one teacher. It's not practical to custom-design a curriculum for each student. Nor could even the most skilled and engaged teacher know each student as intimately as their respective parents. We *know* our kids! We know their personalities, strengths, weaknesses, fears, talents, and everything that makes them unique. The best teachers on the planet cannot possibly know our kids in this way, and we can't expect them to.

Additionally, in a group-school environment (i.e., traditional classroom) we all know that there are a variety of aptitudes and needs amongst the students. It makes sense that a "standard" should be developed to teach and measure the progression of particular age groups. Both public and private schools share this same model, which is really the only practical way to teach a large, disparate group of students simultaneously. This traditional group-school model works well to manage this logistics problem but is lacking in terms of addressing individual student strengths and weaknesses. When homeschooling, the logistics problem doesn't exist, and individual needs can be strategically met.

Once I realized we didn't need to recreate the traditional classroom, and that we could customize our kids' education, I discovered a new type of freedom. As mentioned, my wife and I have near-perfect knowledge of our kids' strengths and weaknesses. We know when they are really trying or just being lazy. We know them and can customize their education for the unique way they are wired. Imagine eliminating all the inefficiencies inherent in the traditional school model; the commute, the drama, the daily scramble — the homework! I encourage you to reflect on what that might look like for your family.

This isn't a how-to book, so I'll just mention that the process of customizing our kids' education was not painful or overly time-consuming. We periodically reevaluate activities, curriculum, and make adjustments as needed. That doesn't mean starting from scratch every semester (you can, of course, but don't have to). Often, there are just small tweaks that can make things more efficient or further challenge the kids. My old skeptical self would never have believed it, but I now look forward to planning each new school year!

But how will I know if my kids are on track for their grade? That's a question asked by every skeptical homeschool dad. Standardized tests are one way to gauge your kids' proficiency in core subjects, compared to their peers. There are many other ways also, such as following the guidelines and testing provided by free or paid curricula.

A common misconception is that homeschool students

can't take standardized tests. This is false. In most school districts, the schools will make the standardized test available for your kids to take along with the public-school students. States and school districts vary in how and when, but if you want your kids tested they can be. Standardized testing is generally optional for homeschoolers (check with your state). I've used standardized tests as one of several tools and found them to be useful measures of academic strengths and possible weaknesses.

It's been widely reported that homeschool students consistently do better than their traditionally schooled peers on their standardized test scores. It's important to me that my kids are at or above the level they should be for their grade in core subject areas, so my family utilizes standardized tests to help gauge this.

How do homeschoolers compare to their traditionally schooled peers? One of the most extensive studies ever conducted of homeschooler's standardized test scores found them to be 37% higher than those of average public school students.

> Surveying 11,739 homeschooling students and their families from all 50 states through 15 independent testing services, Homeschool Progress Report 2009: Academic Achievement and Demographics is the most comprehensive study of homeschool academic achievement to date. The results support the large existing body of research on homeschool academic

achievement and show homeschoolers, on average, scoring 37 percentile points above public school students on standardized achievement tests. The study also found that the achievement gaps common to public schools were practically insignificant in the homeschool community. Conducted by Dr. Brian Ray of the National Home Education Research Institute.

Homeschool Progress Report 2009: Academic Achievement and Demographics. Accessed June 27, 2018. https://eric.ed.gov/?id=ED535134.

I find those statistics to be impressive, particularly since traditional schools increasingly "teach to the test." The full report includes some additional eye-opening demographics findings.

Like many families in the homeschooling world, we don't gear our kids' studies strictly according to grade. We follow the state requirements for subjects certainly, but we let each of our kids' strengths run while shoring up their weaknesses. This means, for example, our third grader is never limited to merely 3rd grade curriculum. Home-schooling means there are no artificial limitations placed on our kids nor on us.

What about SAT scores?

Studies have shown that homeschooled high school students continue to significantly outscore their peers.

The SAT 2014 test scores of college-bound homeschool students were higher than the national average of all college-bound seniors that same year. Some 13,549 homeschool seniors had the following mean scores: 567 in critical reading, 521 in mathematics, and 535 in writing (College Board, 2014a). The mean SAT scores for all college-bound seniors in 2014 were 497 in critical reading, 513 in mathematics, and 487 in writing (College Board, 2014b).

Homeschool SAT Scores for 2014 Higher Than National Average. Accessed June 27, 2018.   https://www.nheri.org/homeschool-sat-scores-for-2014-higher-than-national-average.

Bottom Line

Academic excellence is something we all want for our kids. I was very concerned about this both before and after we made the decision to homeschool. My experience with homeschooling, however, has allowed the freedom to provide *customized* academic options for our kids. Options that are just not possible in the traditional classroom where individual strengths and weaknesses are often neglected.

Standardized testing and other objective measures provide a gauge of our kids' progress along the way for their grade levels.

FOUR

Can't Go to A Good College

I WAS convinced homeschooling would be the kiss of death for college admissions – at least for entry into any reputable, accredited institution. I admit that to the uninformed, this myth sounds credible.

I could clearly picture the admissions process in my head. The smoke-filled room (as if there were still places that allow indoor smoking) full of admissions administrators, the gatekeepers of my child's future. I imagined them laughing at my son's transcript – which was basically a note from mom stating, "junior did a great job on his studies" and how we "couldn't be prouder of our big boy." Of course, I imagined a painfully awkward photo attached, depicting a disheveled, non-socialized boy wearing braces with full headgear! This nightmare ends with the admissions counselors laughing profusely as they mock my family and me, concluding that I should be in jail for ruining my kid's life. Yep, that's how the scenario played in my mind before I learned the truth. Thankfully, my investigation proved it false.

In reality, this myth doesn't even apply to most home-schoolers. This is because many, possibly most, kids who are homeschooled ultimately attend traditional high schools. One advantage is the student has a transcript from a "regular" school and funnels into the standard college admissions process just like everyone else. Their home-schooled history isn't a negative factor in their college application. I want to be clear, this is not the basis on which I would recommend deciding whether to home-school your child through high school. I'm just pointing out that if you do choose the traditional high school route, the myth becomes a non-issue.

Irrespective of the high school choice, the early home-schooled years will have provided expanded life-experi-ences and achievements that will *help* your kids stand out amongst other college applicants. We all know it takes more than just a high GPA and high SAT scores to get into the better colleges. Extra-curricular achievements are increasingly crucial for differentiation. The breadth of the homeschooling experience provides tons of genuinely valu-able educational experiences and opportunities for devel-opment. Don't be too quick to discount the positive and differentiating effect of these experiences.

Homeschooled for High School

For those families that continue homeschooling through high school, the transcript and grades are a genuine concern — they just won't be weighed in the same manner as if they had been issued by a traditional high school. But this is not a show-stopper! The reality is that colleges are more open to homeschoolers than they've ever been. This is a good trend, and one that I think will likely continue.

Some of the more innovative schools, such as Stanford and Princeton Universities, have actually developed specific admissions process for homeschooled students. Many other institutions have made similar moves to attract homeschooled students. You're certainly not limited to colleges that have a separate homeschool admissions process, but it's an encouraging trend. It shows that colleges want to attract homeschooled students. This means they have seen something in them that is worth attracting. They want them (at least the best ones) in their student body.

I think the following statement from the MIT online admissions page nicely summarizes the qualities home-schoolers can and must demonstrate:

> One quality that we look for in all of our applicants is evidence of having taken initiative, showing an entrepreneurial spirit, taking full advantage of opportunities. Many of our admitted homeschooled

applicants really shine in this area. These students truly take advantage of their less constrained educational environment to take on exciting projects, go in depth in topics that excite them, create new opportunities for themselves and others, and more.

Homeschooled Students | MIT Admissions. Deadlines & Requirements. Accessed June 27, 2018. http://mitadmissions.org/apply/prepare/homeschool.

It's one thing for the Ivy League liberal arts schools to recognize the value in homeschooling, but for MIT to demonstrate that it, too, understands and values attracting homeschooled students reflects a fundamental change in thinking. The above quote demonstrates that home-schooled students are gaining admission and are thriving in the best, most competitive colleges in the country. This is a paradigm shift.

Bottom Line

For most families, this myth doesn't apply. Don't make the decision about homeschooling your 3rd grader now, based on myths and fears that aren't a factor until high school. If you're in the elementary or middle school stages of life, this myth doesn't apply to you.

It is true, however, that students who are homeschooled for the high school grades need to significantly differentiate themselves. The good news is there are many ways to achieve this, and the homeschool process naturally lends itself to more significant and differentiating experiences than can be provided by most traditional schools. *Home-schooled high school students are indeed getting into good schools.* They stand out by *actually doing* many things that the traditionally schooled applicants have only read about.

As stated earlier, colleges are increasingly "friendly" to homeschooled high schoolers with some even implementing custom admissions processes for this group. The concern is that other colleges may be biased against the homeschooler. If your child goes to traditional public or private high school (or perhaps one of the hybrid or charter programs), this problem is avoided. If you choose to homeschool through high school, then this bias must be addressed by the *proven* life-experience, life-skills, communication skills, and other tangible achievements. As shown, the best colleges are expecting this type of differentiation among homeschooled applicants — and in many cases finding it.

FIVE

Miss the School Experience

IN MY MIND, the myth of missed experiences conjured images of my kids sitting at home, in pajamas, basking in the awkwardness and solitude of unsocialized homeschool life. No friends. No knowledge of the culture outside the walls of our house. No life-shaping experiences. A small and lackluster existence that would deprive them of all that's good in life. And it would be my fault for letting it happen!

The idea that my kids would miss out on significant life-experiences was something that, for me, made the concept of homeschooling unthinkable. Why would I rob my kids of such exciting and notable events like football games, proms, student government, graduation, and even the rollercoaster ride of social development and popularity? We all can agree that while not *all* school experiences are positive, we don't want our kids to miss out on the good ones.

I know the current trend in traditional public elementary and middle schools is the reduction or elimination of the programs that once provided the "experiences" we want for our kids. It's increasingly rare for schools to offer such things as field trips, camps, music, art, and sports teams. Maybe your local district is different, I hope it is. But this is the sad reality in most school districts.

Homeschooling does not have these limitations. My kids participate in life-enriching activities several days per week, and it's even possible to use charter school funds to pay for some or all of it. Traditional schools are brick and mortar institutions that are expensive to operate and to staff. There just isn't enough money for anything "extra" anymore. But the "extra" is what makes the experience rich. It connects what our kids learn to the real world in many ways. It's also part of what develops a cultured, three-dimensional person. Homeschooling is free from the overhead (financial and bureaucratic) of the brick and mortar institutions. The actual cost for us to educate our kids is far less than it costs for a traditional school to do so meaning that we have the time and money left over to pack our weeks with incredible experiences.

Initially, when my wife and I made the decision to try homeschooling, we were a bit green and still concerned about some of the common myths — socialization and missed experiences, in particular. We feared that our kids' "school experience" would be *smaller* in some way than that of their peers. Though convinced we could offer them a better overall academic learning experience, we mistakenly believed it would have to come at the price of their social experience. Since both types of experiences are crucial, we found ourselves in a bit of a dilemma. Instead of allowing our fears to stop us, we explored other ways that our kids could gain *bigger and more significant* social experiences. We believed the myth that our kids would miss out on the "school experience" — it turned out to be just the opposite.

I had no idea when we first started just how *big* the homeschooling experience would be. My wife enrolled us in a local co-op which meets one day per week. I've mentioned this elsewhere, but in case you jumped directly to this section, it's a group of around 100 families that includes kids of all ages, even through high school. It's no Amish schoolhouse! Our kids get to take a vast variety of classes taught by accomplished parents and professional teachers. Additionally, the co-op sponsors weekly field trips, beach days, park days, dances, and family events.

Needless to say, we were busy. But that didn't stop us from adding even more. I won't bore you with a long list of additional classes and activities, but I've found the *hardest thing about homeschooling has been the realization that we can't do everything* that is available to us! Our kids are outside, with people, experiencing the world in a hands-on way. They have lots of *big* experiences — way more than they would spending 6 or 7 hours inside a classroom with the same 30 kids every day!

The myth of missed experiences also harkens back to the related fears regarding lack of socialization and isolation. Because some have stereotyped homeschooled kids as unsocialized and isolated, it is assumed they will miss out on "all the cool stuff" that comes with the "school experience." For elementary and middle school kids, I've found the academic and social homeschool experience can be much bigger than that of traditional school.

I encourage you, as a dad, to make the best choice for each kid at *each season of life*. And yes, that means an ongoing evaluation of their education options. If your son or daughter isn't getting the types of experiences they need at a given age or in a particular environment, make a change! You have that power. If traditional schooling isn't working well in this season, give homeschooling a try. If homeschooling isn't working for you, then switch back to traditional schooling.

The High School Experience

Now, the myth of missing out on the school experience *can* be true for high schoolers, though it doesn't have to be! High school is a special period in adolescent life. We all want our kids to have a great, positive "high school experience." It can be an exciting time and a time of important personal growth. Parents of both traditional and home-schooled students agree on this point.

I have not yet personally raised high schoolers, so I can only share what I have observed with the families in our community. Many families enroll their previously home-schooled kids into public or private traditional high schools. Many others choose one of the hybrid programs that offer a combination of on-campus and independent learning programs. The hybrid programs can provide many academic and social opportunities like those of traditional high schools.

As I've mentioned, there's a growing trend to home-school through high school which provides yet another viable option. Many of these families take advantage of dual enrollment which allows high schoolers to take college courses at their local junior college. There are many benefits to this option including earning college credits, demonstrating academic competence, and college cost savings. These classes are typically offered online by local community colleges. Be sure to also see the "High School Sports" section of the "Can't Play Team Sports" chapter to find out how homeschoolers can often participate in local high school team sports and other activities.

The dads of homeschooled high schoolers consistently affirm that we must be willing to choose the option that will be best overall for each of our kids — there will be tradeoffs, and no option will be perfect. These dads have made tough, often unpopular decisions. For some, the choice is to continue homeschooling through the high school grades. For others, the transition to traditional high school might be best. In either case, some valuable opportunities will be compromised. As the homeschooling movement continues to grow, so do the type of activities that were previously available only through traditional high schools. For example, many co-ops provide dances, yearbooks, and student government. On a bigger scale, there are large regional or statewide home-school organizations that successfully bridge the gap between traditional high school activities and those available to local homeschoolers. These organizations attract homeschooled students from broader geographic areas to participate in activities that include sports, dances (including proms), academic competitions, and graduation ceremonies.

You may be shocked to learn homeschooled high schoolers turn out fine. If you put a bunch of high schoolers in a room, I don't think you'd be able to tell the difference between those who were homeschooled and those who were not. It's entirely possible for kids to be quirky or cool given either option. Remember, home-schooled kids have friends and socialize (and get into their share of trouble) too!

Bottom Line

If we make a choice to homeschool our kids during any season of their education, it's our responsibility to make sure they have a rich and "big" experience. This is just as true if we send them to traditional schools as it is if we choose to homeschool. Either way, we dads need to be purposeful and strategic about providing the best possible experiences, those that will shape our kids in positive and meaningful ways.

Myths About Limitations of Parents

SIX

I'm Not Equipped to Teach

MY MIND WENT IMMEDIATELY to an image of myself standing in front of a group of unruly kids, struggling to explain the quadratic equation scribbled in white chalk on a slate blackboard from the early 1970's. I honestly don't remember the quadratic equation, only the name because it was connected to so much anxiety when I was a student during the previous millennium. Now, I'm not sure why my vision had me teaching this to my kids, but I have an active imagination, so here I found myself. Oh, and there were 10 kids present — not sure why, since I only have two. But nonetheless, my imagination was trying to make the point that I was not equipped to teach! As I envisioned trying to explain the math lesson, I felt an authentic sense of inadequacy. A desire to run from this. The feeling that failure was imminent. Now, that's a heavy set of emotions and fears to stream from a half-lucid daydream. But math has a way of conjuring those frightful emotions in me! Maybe in you, too. Or perhaps it's the teaching of a different subject that makes you uncomfortable.

I think all of us entertain some variation of this fear — and thus believe the myth. I can hear the protests of skeptical dads, "But I'm not equipped to teach advanced math or science." I'm not either. This myth, however, makes a huge leap of logic. It infers that if I can't teach advanced math or chemistry, I can't teach anything! Actually, I'm perfectly capable of instructing my elementary aged daughter in how to add numbers. I can help her sound-out a difficult word in a book. But belief in this myth causes us to project our feelings of inadequacy into all areas of our kids' education process. The myth that I'm not equipped to teach is actually the myth that I'm not equipped to be in control of my kids' education. That I should surrender all of it to the professionals. Just who do I think I am, after all?

Sometimes when dealing with myths, it's helpful to focus more on the conclusions we draw from them. For example, there is truth to the statement that we may not be equipped to teach *everything.* But that's not a problem because we can teach some things, and use curricula, classes, and workshops as necessary for the rest. In fact, homeschooling does not require you to *teach* in the traditional classroom sense at all (unless you want to).

My previously mentioned fears about teaching my kids the quadratic equation might have been sufficient reason to abandon the homeschooling idea entirely. But I now know that I don't have to be the one to teach it to them. We have access to teacher-led classes, online courses, and book-based curricula that are effective at teaching every level of math. These are readily available at little to no cost. For example, the math curriculum we use does a great job of explaining the quadratic equation, why it exists and how it's utilized.

A big part of our personal homeschooling methodology is to foster resourcefulness. When my kids have questions about a subject, they aren't allowed to just ask me for help. They first need to try to find the answer or solve the problem themselves. If they become stuck, I might recommend additional resources or engage with them in the search, but I don't just give them the answers. My role is much more that of mentor than teacher.

Remember, homeschoolers aren't teaching a classroom full of other people's kids. They are teaching (mentoring) their own kids. Of course, many useful tools and curricula are available for every grade level and subject, but none requires us to stand in front of a chalkboard or behind a podium. What I'm saying is that the type of homeschool "teaching" you likely envision is not reality.

In a traditional group-school environment, we need professional teachers. The specialized training they receive is necessary because they teach a lot of kids a variety of subjects. They have to deal with all kinds of behavioral and learning challenges with kids at various levels of ability. I would not be equipped to teach a classroom full of other people's kids! But the reality is I'm *not* teaching a classroom full of other people's kids. I'm only teaching my own kids. And *I'm not recreating the classroom*. This changes everything and makes it very manageable.

Bottom Line

Homeschooling provides the freedom to structure your kids' education however you'd like. You can employ whatever is best for them during that season. That's the whole point of homeschooling — customized education!

I've found that it took some time to become comfortable with the freedom that we have when we homeschool. It feels foreign at first because we've only known the traditional, group-school model. Once you realize what you *can* do for your kids, a new world opens up. Not in an overwhelming way, but in an empowering way.

SEVEN

Daunting, I Don't Know Where to Start

I JUST DON'T KNOW where to start. My wife and I said that many times both before and after we made the decision to homeschool. This is such a prevailing sentiment that it alone keeps a lot of people from honestly investigating the homeschooling option. Looking back, I don't know why the idea of homeschooling was so scary. Perhaps it was because I believed a bunch of myths.

When we decided to begin homeschooling, we felt ill-equipped and that we needed to learn a few things before getting started. Our timing was right because California's largest homeschooling convention was coming to town. We dropped the kids at their grandparent's house for the day and headed off to the convention. We were newbies but expected to return as experts. Bear in mind, we were still skeptical about the homeschool movement and our ability to manage it.

I actually wanted an excuse that would give me permission to abandon this crazy idea that I could better manage my kids' education — permission to remain in what felt comfortable and safe. We stayed and listened to several of the speakers, all of whom were outstanding! Great communicators, funny, informative, and surprisingly…cool. So many stereotypes were starting to give way to a new reality. I started feeling like homeschooling might not be so hard after all. But I had yet to encounter the "vendor room."

We had heard that this convention would provide an excellent opportunity to see and evaluate a lot of curricula and other learning aids. That sounded good, and I wrongly assumed that we'd walk away from the convention with all the materials we'd need. But when we entered the "vendor room," my jaw dropped. It was a huge convention center room packed to the gills with booth after booth full of workbooks, DVDs, school supplies, interactive classes, learning aids, hands-on projects, lesson planners, crafts, books, and…pretty much anything school-related that you can imagine. It felt like there were tens of thousands of vendors. We quite literally didn't know where to start. And honestly, I wasn't sure that I even wanted to.

This barrage of curricula turned me off for many reasons. The task ahead of me, to figure out which of these curricula options would work for our kids and how we would manage their use of it, was indeed daunting. The presumption that we would need to figure this out for every subject and for each kid seemed impossible — or so we thought. Then there was the expense of it all! I felt over-whelmed and discouraged. Maybe, I thought to myself, this homeschooling thing is more than we want to tackle. Maybe it's more than we *can* tackle. Back then, we believed that we had to buy curriculum for each subject, then "teach" each subject every day — per kid! Thankfully, that turned out not to be the case. Don't get me wrong, some homeschoolers do it that way but not most. And none have to. More on that later. But I didn't know any better at the time, so the "daunting-ness" of it all was fully manifested, realized, and validated at that single moment.

Another reason I didn't like what I saw in the "vendor room," was that I hated the idea of my kids spending their days heads-down in worksheets or watching some boring lecture on DVD. Inside. Isolated. All the previously dispelled fears came flooding back. How could those be avoided if we were spending all day in this or that curriculum? To me, that was worse than spending 6 hours in class every day.

Thankfully, we found an abundance of better options that did not require tons of curricula nor excessive time spent heads-down working through countless worksheets. These better options included classes and learning activities made available by our co-op, weekly field trips, and theater workshops. We do use formal curricula for specific subjects, such as math. I never would have believed it in the beginning, but the management of all these options has proven to be easy.

Initially, I had assumed homeschooling would require a burdensome amount of tracking and reporting. It had to, I reasoned, thinking about the massive bureaucracy that is the US education system. I envisioned piles of paper, my wife frazzled as she pulled all-nighters to get grades and attendance submitted to some government regulatory body. Thankfully, that's not the case at all. Sure, there are requirements that homeschoolers must follow, but they are minimal, and not burdensome.

I was pleasantly surprised by the lack of "administrivia" we had to contend with. There was no governing body to which we must report. No person assigned to oversee our activities. We are accountable to the state regarding the academic subjects that must be taught but are free to satisfy those requirements however we see fit. It's not daunting; it's freedom!

I have since experienced homeschooling both independently and also partnering with charter schools. Both are easy. Setting up as an independent homeschool was as simple as filing a form online. Then we were off to the races (figuratively, of course). Likewise, partnering with a charter school was almost as simple. There are a few additional requirements when working with a charter school because as a public school, they must satisfy additional state requirements. Again, it was not burdensome. For many new homeschoolers, working with a charter school alleviates much of the anxiety surrounding the process because the charter school provides oversight and student record administration.

What does a typical homeschool week look like for my family? We like to focus on core academic subjects at home. This keeps the kids focused, and we can monitor (not micromanage) their work times. This helps keep their workloads manageable because we aren't incurring homework from external classes. They get their work completed relatively quickly (usually without much prodding) freeing the remainder of the day for other activities.

We utilize external classes and workshops to foster creativity and further develop communications skills in group settings. Group field trips, often multiple days per week, provide hands-on experiences and meaningful social interaction. Music and theater play a recurring role in the schedule, as does volleyball. Each of these classes meet only once per week, not daily. Therefore, the kids are doing different things each day. Scheduling is easy because we set it all up at the start of each semester.

If the schedule I've described sounds daunting to you, it's probably because you're accustomed to working these types of activities around the typical school day. What if all those hours devoted to traditional school each week were given back to you? Just think of how many worthwhile, enriching activities your kids would have the time and energy to do.

Bottom Line

These are my kids. I know them better than anyone. They have been entrusted to me. Daunting or not, I decided I would do whatever was needed to give them the best possible education. That decision took a surprising amount of courage. Going in, I fully expected homeschooling to be hard. But as it turned out, aside from navigating the "vendor room" at the homeschooling convention, getting started was not a daunting task at all!

EIGHT

I Don't Have Time

I WAS ALREADY BUSY, really busy! At the time we first discussed the possibility of homeschooling, I was working crazy hours in a technology start-up that I co-founded. I didn't have the option of adding anything new to my plate. Homeschooling would make me busier, I assumed, which was a good reason not to do it! Case closed, or so I thought. I get it, most of us don't have enough time for the commitments we already have. None of us wants to add more to our respective plates.

However, it turns out homeschooling *can actually make you less busy* and your life way less hectic. I know that's a nonintuitive statement, but it's true. And the actual myth, that homeschooling inherently makes you busier, adding additional overhead to your already packed task list, is false. But here's the rub; notice I said that it *can* result in less busyness. Some people like to go 100 MPH all the time piling on activity upon activity. You can certainly do that while homeschooling, just like you can if your kids are in traditional school. But the difference is when homeschooling, you don't have to. This is because you're in control and can orchestrate your "school" and schedule any way you see fit.

I've found the crazy-busy life of most families is significantly due to the demands of the school system itself. Between the daily pick-up and drop-off routine (potentially at multiple schools), morning scramble to get everybody ready and make sure they have all they need for the day, and the nightly homework routine, it's surprising anyone stays sane. Added to this is the myriad of the extracurricular sports, music, dance, supplemental academics, church, social, and service activities.

Let's get real for a minute. As a fellow dad, I suspect you're worried about homeschooling demands overflowing onto your plate. I did too. When we started homeschooling, my wife and I agreed she would manage the schooling, and I'd manage the business — it's not sexist, just the way we chose to divide and conquer the responsibilities of our family life. But I was pretty sure that the new "burdens" of homeschooling would be more than one person could handle and expected to have to pick up a lot of slack. In the next chapter, we'll tackle the corresponding myth "My Wife Will Be Overwhelmed."

Like you, I'm continuously fighting to delegate or otherwise eliminate tasks. I need less on my plate, not more! Even after I was sold on the idea of homeschooling, I worried about the impact on my schedule. I won't lie there are times when it's inconvenient, when I do need to pick up the slack. I'm not suggesting it's always perfect — nothing is! But overall, I am *personally* less burdened by school-related tasks and the associated franticness than I was when the kids were in traditional school. I don't know any homeschoolers who miss the constant shuttling of kids to and from schools, waiting in long lines to drop-off or pick-up. The endless and excessive homework. Late nights and early mornings. For my family, life is calmer now, saner. And so are the kids.

I do spend time engaged in my kids' education. I sometimes even invest time and energy into activities that I wouldn't have, were we part of a traditional school. The crucial takeaway is that I've *chosen* to do this because I have found it to be meaningful and worthwhile for my kids and me. I also get to attend many field trips and events with my family. I don't have to, there's no requirement that I attend, but I now have an empowered outlook on my role in the education process.

You might be reading this and thinking, "I don't have the time nor the desire to attend school activities." Then don't. I'm trying to convey that seeing my kids learn, grow, and thrive *became* exciting to me — something I want to be part of whenever I can. *Homeschooling doesn't make you busier by default.* You can create a schedule and strategy that works for your family with built-in margin and participate along with your kids when you want to.

Lastly, I want to mention an *unintended* benefit of home-schooling that skeptical dads will appreciate. We now have the freedom to schedule vacations whenever we'd like. We can travel off-season, taking advantage of significantly reduced rates and flexible bookings. Let's face it, Disney-land is much more enjoyable on a Tuesday in February than it is on a sold-out Saturday in July! A trip to Europe in April will be much more affordable and the famous sites less crowded than the same trip in August.

Bottom Line

The myth that homeschooling inherently makes you busier is not true. My experience has been that my family is less busy (but more active), overall. This has been our choice. We have made the conscious effort to maintain margin in our schedule, but it doesn't happen by accident. We get to make this choice because we're in control.

Indeed, homeschooling brought freedom from the tedium and tyranny of the traditional school's schedule. My entire family now has time for more important things. We are plenty busy these days, I won't pretend otherwise. But we are busy with activities that we've *chosen* because they are *worthwhile*. We aren't recreating the traditional classroom at home, and our kids are learning to be resourceful, learning how to teach themselves. My family has found freedom in homeschooling in every conceivable way.

NINE

My Wife Will Be Overwhelmed

OVERWHELM IS a fear of many skeptical dads. Because I had no idea how much work homeschooling might be, I expected the worst. Basically, we assume our wives will become overwhelmed by the sheer number of unanticipated tasks, tedious recordkeeping, and child behavior management to name just a few of the proverbial straws that break the camel's back. My brother once expressed the nature of this myth best when he said, half-jokingly, "My wife will come to hate the children, and then she'll hate me." That statement represents a fair summary of my early fears about homeschooling.

I'm embarrassed to admit that I was not merely worried about my wife. Let's face it, if she becomes overwhelmed, things are going to spill over onto my already full plate. For most of us, that's a pretty good excuse not to tackle homeschooling. Worse yet, if she's stressed out, discouraged, and otherwise spent, I'm not likely to get any action! And that's an *excellent* reason not to homeschool!

Thankfully, the overwhelm never occurred, and my worst fears didn't manifest. Let me be clear that *homeschooling doesn't inherently lead to an overwhelmed life*. But be warned, it could if you're not careful!

The myth is one that can become a reality if you think you need to "do school" at home by trying to recreate the classroom. Homeschooling can also get overwhelming if you say yes to every great opportunity that comes along. Like I've said repeatedly, homeschooling puts you in the driver's seat. How fast or slow you drive, and where you choose to go is up to you.

When families first start homeschooling, they discover countless great adventures and classes and field trips and other opportunities available for their kids to take part in. Once we began homeschooling (and our days were freed from the tyranny of the 6-hour indoor school days), we discovered a vast world of adventure, exploration, creativity, and hands-on education — and *we wanted to do all of it!* In fact, we initially felt that we *had* to do all of it! I will tell you up front, you don't have to. And you can't! If some homeschool families go through a season of "overwhelm" it's most likely due to over commitment.

Bottom Line

If you choose the homeschooling option, you'll need to determine a make-sense schedule based on your own family dynamics and energy levels. Let's face it, some people like to go 100 MPH all the time and try to do it all. Others are better suited to something less hectic. The main takeaway here is that you can avoid becoming overwhelmed by customizing your schedule and commitments to your liking. Furthermore, you can change it up, adjusting whenever you need to. If you find that you or your wife are getting frazzled, you can pull back. After all, you're in the driver's seat.

TEN

We Can't Afford It, and We Already Paid for School Through Taxation

I'VE HEARD GUYS SAY, "I need to use the public education system, I've paid for it!" It's true that you've already paid for your "free" public education through taxation. I don't dispute that at all.

But the myth is that we *must utilize the institution that we were forced to pay for*. Actually, no one is forcing you to use the public education system. Homeschoolers and traditional private schoolers are in the same boat here. Those who have chosen private schooling for their kids also had to debunk this myth.

Complaints about excessive taxes are part of the mantra of many a skeptical dad. I get it. For our entire "earning" life we pay to fund the education system. In the US we are required to pay via taxation for every child to have a free government-provided education. That free education turns out to be quite expensive. Those of us who choose an alternative, such as private school, are then paying for schooling twice!

Early on, this really got me riled up (taxes have a way of doing that anyhow). "Really," I thought, "I'm considering paying out-of-pocket, with after-tax dollars, for something I've already paid for?" That sounds absurd.

It took a while, but I finally came to terms with the fact that the monies I was forced to pay through taxes must not be a factor in the decision. I must first determine the best education option then figure out how to pay for it. If public school is the best option in the end, then we don't need to worry about the sunk cost of our taxes. But what if homeschooling is the best option?

In a handful of states, some of our tax dollars *can be* leveraged for certain homeschooling expenses through charter schools. But even if they can't, we ultimately must do what's best for our kids.

Skeptical dads also tend to embrace a related myth that homeschooling is expensive. It's not, but I can understand why guys might think so. Traditional schools seem to be continuously engaged in fund-raising efforts. Activities such as team sports, music, and field trips are increasingly being eliminated due to budget shortfalls. Teachers fear for their jobs and retirement. All of this despite the massive amount of tax dollars flowing into the education system. The infrastructure required to support mass education is expensive. Homeschooling avoids these infrastructure and other expenses entirely.

Homeschooling is not expensive — at least it need not be. Again, you are in the driver's seat. You can choose costly educational options, or you can enroll in free or almost free classes, events, and other activities. For example, our co-op involvement is practically free, yet it provides many classes, social events, field trips, and dances. Additionally, we spend very little on curriculum, and most of the books on our reading list are either free digitally or available at the library.

Bottom Line

I think perspective is vital when evaluating this concern. Taxation is an obligation. And it's a sunk cost. We must pay taxes toward the education system whether we utilize it or not. That reality, however, does not *obligate us* to use the system we are required to fund. The goal is for our kids to receive the best possible education — not merely to get our money's worth from the taxes we pay. Once I came to terms with this idea, I was free to evaluate my options with an open mind. I still don't like it, but I've moved past it.

ELEVEN

We Will Be Labeled Kooks

HOMESCHOOLING IS no longer considered a fringe movement in most parts of the US. I would go so far as to say it's becoming almost trendy in some areas. Due to its increasing popularity over the past several years, I no longer get as many suspicious looks when I tell people that we homeschool. These days, the myth that our family will be labeled as kooks, or that our choice to homeschool will be perceived as irresponsible, is false. Besides, we dads like to think we're above caring about what others think. The truth is that we aren't.

Homeschooling usually comes up in conversation because people ask, "so, where do your kids go to school?" As a new homeschooler, I was always eager to answer this question because it provided an opening to share the new world of opportunities we were experiencing. Excitedly, I would reply, "We homeschool." Then silence, sometimes followed by a painfully contorted facial expression and a condescending, "Really?" Other times my statement would be met by a rapid-fire series of "gotcha" type pseudo-questions — not sincere, but rather chosen to point out my kookiness. These always began with the mother of all homeschool questions, "Well, what about socialization?" Of course, we've already debunked that myth in the "What About Socialization?" chapter. It's the attitude behind the question that I want to focus on here.

There still exists an attitude among some people that homeschoolers are willing to compromise what's best for our kids out of the zealous pursuit of some fringe belief system. While I can't speak for every homeschool family, I can state confidently I've never seen that to be the case. We aren't joining a cult, we're just choosing a different model for education. We aren't embracing an Amish lifestyle, we are merely finding ways for our kids to experience the world and learn beyond the confines of the traditional classroom box. The important takeaway is that we are choosing to pursue the options we think are best for our kids, not compromising their wellbeing.

People are sometimes quick to believe stupid things that fit their biases. It was almost comical to me that some people assumed I'd never given thought to questions such as "socialization" before betting my kids' education on it. They also assumed there couldn't possibly be good answers to such questions. Hence, the danger of believing myths. Now, people weren't typically rude or mean, but when I provided answers to some of these questions, those listening often interrupted and move straight to the common assertion, "That's great for you, but it would never work for me." This will be the next myth we debunk.

Today, thankfully, the conversations go a bit differently. When people find out that we homeschool, the response I get is usually one of sincere interest regarding how it's going and whether we plan to proceed through the upper grades. I don't want to paint too rosy a picture since there are a lot of skeptics out there. I've found that people still ask about many of the myths surrounding homeschooling which continue to propagate, but increasingly it's because they genuinely want to understand. I very rarely get the barrage of "gotcha" questions anymore.

You might find it interesting to hear what our close friends and family members thought when we told them we had decided to homeschool. They probably thought we'd gone a bit crazy. But they loved us anyhow, and we all survived it. Since we've been doing it a while now, most of those who were skeptical, and probably thought we'd ruin our kids or burnout and return to traditional school, have become genuinely interested in our results and progress.

My wife and I were quite confident in our decision to homeschool. However, there was one person to whom I feared having to explain our decision, my father. You must understand, he was a career educator. He taught inner-city junior high early in his career and later as a professor at an internationally renowned university. At the time of his retirement, he was Dean of one of the premier business schools in the US. Needless to say, our choice to go rogue with the education of *his grandchildren* would not likely go unopposed. Oh, I forgot to mention he's also a lawyer! You probably assume, like I did, that this conversation might go poorly. But, spoiler alert, it didn't! However, that doesn't mean it was an easy conversation to have.

He listened intently as I presented my best case for why we could do a better job of educating his grandchildren than professional educators. Why our model would yield better results than those of the education system which had educated members of civilized society for hundreds of years. His furled brow was disturbingly familiar and reminiscent of scoldings I'd received growing up. Not childhood scoldings mind you, but those from my teenage years when I was in *real* trouble.

After listening to me for a time, he asked sternly, "Is there some sort of accredited board or organization that will provide oversite?" I paused, and sheepishly answered, "No." Then I waited for the crash of the gavel — but it never came. Instead, he asked some quite pointed but reasonable questions, to which my wife and I had surprisingly good answers. I felt like I'd actually made a decent case for homeschooling, having debunked many of the same myths that I've included in this book. In the end, my father was intrigued by some of the options that we explained. Like me, he was surprised to learn that the myths he believed about homeschooling were not true.

He's continued to watch our journey closely and witnessed his grandchildren thrive. He's also seen how good it's been for my wife and me.

In the end, presenting a case for homeschooling to my professor-father was a significant milestone. Sharing the pros and cons of the homeschooling option to one who I knew would be skeptical and critical forced me to objectively evaluate all that I believed to be true about it. My wife and I didn't need anyone else's permission to home-school our kids — we are the ones entrusted with the stewardship of them. But we did, and do, care what certain people think — because we know they love us, and we value their wisdom.

Bottom Line

Will you be labeled a kook by some if you choose to home-school your kids? Perhaps. But less today than in previous years. You should expect some ribbing and probing questions from friends and family. But in the end, who cares? As dads, we need to do the right thing for our family — regardless of what others think. Debunking those myths to which we still cling is the first step to making the best decision.

TWELVE

It Just Won't Work for Us

WE'VE DEBUNKED a lot of myths in this book, 11 big ones so far. This final myth serves as a type of "catch-all" assertion about homeschooling. When all else fails, skeptical dads (and skeptical moms) like to throw this one out to abruptly end discussions about homeschooling. It's like saying, "I have many good reasons, but I don't want to share them, and I don't want to talk about it anymore."

I purposely placed this myth last because it's often the last resort for skeptical dads who don't want to further discuss the topic. It's not a reason-based statement but rather an emotional reaction. Skeptical dads state that "it just won't work" when they are out of arguments and feel backed into a corner. This puts an immediate stop to the conversation using a purely subjective assertion rather than a well-reasoned argument. Now, if you responded this way to me in a discussion, I'd drop it — you don't owe me an explanation, and it's frankly not anyone else's business anyhow. But when it's your wife trying to understand why you aren't willing to investigate the homeschooling option, *you absolutely do owe her a thoughtful explanation!*

As I mentioned earlier, I've found that skeptical moms also believe this myth. But they mean something different when they say it. They usually mean they personally are not equipped to tackle homeschooling. I've heard skeptical moms say things like, "I just don't have the patience" or "My kids would never listen to me." Both are self-limiting statements that stem from insecurities. She might not have the patience, at first, and the kids might not listen to her, at first. But over time, and with Dad's support, mom will develop the patience, the kids will learn to listen, and she'll do a good job. I've seen this transformation happen with many families.

The knee-jerk myth that homeschooling "just won't work for us" is false on its face because there is no reasoning behind it. If you have *actual reasons why it won't work for you,* that's entirely different. If so, what are they? If you wanted it to work, what would you need to do, or give up, to make it happen? I hope you're willing to honestly consider these questions before resorting to this platitude.

Bottom Line

In almost every case, homeschooling can work *if you want it to work.* With the popular myths out of the way, I hope you see that.

The decision to homeschool or not comes down to what you think is best for your kids. That's your decision. Obviously, I think it's the best model for many people, most people even. Yet that doesn't mean it's best for *your* family. But if it were, wouldn't you want to know?

Conclusion

The main reason I wrote this book was to expose and debunk these 12 commonly believed myths surrounding homeschooling. There are many more, of course, that we didn't cover. But I hope you've come away from this book better informed and able to shed these core misconceptions.

I want to end with a word of caution. I have met a lot of women who would love to homeschool. They have performed careful research, spoken to tons of people online and in person, read books, attended open houses, and otherwise done all the necessary legwork to orchestrate a successful homeschool launch for their kids, only to have this effort vetoed by their husbands. Now, I wholeheartedly agree that husbands and wives must be in sync with major decisions regarding their kids' education. One should not make drastic changes without discussion and consensus.

But the consistent story I'm hearing is that husbands *refuse to even consider the idea of homeschooling.* They aren't interested in investigating and discussing what they believe to be a stupid idea. That's a problem. It's one thing to be a skeptical dad. It's another to be an uninformed tyrant.

By reading this book, you have demonstrated that you're at least open-minded. I hope it's paved the way for a thoughtful and informed discussion about the education options available to your kids.

Congratulations, you're at the end of the book — and likely at the end of that beer I encouraged you to grab when we got started. Grab another, you deserve it after wading through the mythology and realities of homeschooling. I wish you well with your education journey, whichever schooling option you choose. And I hope you maximize every moment you have with those amazing kids whose lives have been entrusted to you! Wish I had done so sooner.

Acknowledgments

My wife and I began this homeschooling journey together as skeptics, overcoming these myths as a team. To watch our remarkable kids develop and thrive has been the greatest reward and validation of our efforts. The risks and sacrifices have all been worth it!

This book was indeed a group effort so don't be fooled by the fact that only my name is on the cover. It would not have been possible without the constant support, understanding, and encouragement of my family. I want to thank my wife Dorine for believing in this project and graciously picking up the slack during those times when I sequestered myself to write. Our kids, Asher and Britton, are a constant source of inspiration and confirmation of the importance of a book like this. Thanks for understanding and encouraging me to start and finish this book.

This book would never have come to fruition (or would

not have been intelligible) without the tireless dedication and sacrifice of my editing and beta reader teams: Dorine, Bill, Jo Anne, Marcus, and Allison. Your suggestions, insights, and quality assurance made all the difference.

I'm also indebted to my good friend and fellow home-school sojourner Steve. Your knowledge and insights about homeschooler team sports options and CIF regulations proved invaluable.

A special thanks to the Contemporary Homeschooler (TheContemporaryHomeschooler.com) for writing the foreword to this book. Thank you for freely sharing your wealth of knowledge and empowering homeschoolers everywhere. Your encouragement and example have inspired and emboldened so many to take back the reigns of our kids' education.

About the Author

Kent Larson has been a homeschool dad for most of his kids' educational years. His transformation from antagonist to homeschool advocate was a surprise to many, particularly himself.

Growing up in southern California, Kent augmented his public school education through church, travel, music, and sports. Shortly after college, he discovered a passion for theology and philosophy that he continues to study and write about. Around that same time, he married the love of his life.

Kent has a degree in Economics from Pepperdine

University and has spent more than 25 years as a technology entrepreneur. He is a husband and father living and homeschooling in southern California.

Connect with Kent:

www.kent-larson.com

facebook.com/KentLarsonAuthor

amazon.com/author/kentlarson

goodreads.com/kentlarson

bookbub.com/authors/kent-larson

Free Bonus Content

Most dads are concerned about more than just the 12 primary homeschooling myths that I've chosen to include here. The need to keep this book concise and focused meant that I couldn't cover everything. Many additional myths deserved to be debunked but didn't make the cut. Therefore, I have debunked several additional myths which are available as free bonus content.

Partial List of Bonus Myths

- Things Will Slip Through the Cracks
- It Will Be Expensive
- Can't Go Back to Traditional School
- Kids Will Hate it (and Hate me)

The free bonus content can be obtained by visiting the link below. This is also the place to find information about my additional books and resources.

Get the Free Bonus Content:
www.kent-larson.com/myths-bonus

Thanks for your interest and I hope you find this information helpful as you evaluate education options.

Made in the USA
Middletown, DE
12 March 2019